Crypto and Forex Trading Patterns

Trading in the crypto and forex markets can be challenging, but understanding various trading patterns can help traders make informed decisions and potentially increase their profits.:

Contents

Introduction 1
Head and Shoulders Pattern 2
Inverse Head and Shoulders Pattern 3
Double Top Pattern 4
Double Bottom Pattern 5
Symmetrical Triangle Pattern 6
Descending Triangle Pattern 7
Ascending Triangle Pattern 8
Flag Pattern 9
Pennant Pattern 11
Gartley Pattern 12
Butterfly Pattern 13
Wedge Pattern 14
Rounding Bottom Pattern 16
Rounding Top Pattern 18
Cup and Handle Pattern 19
Channel Pattern 20
Ascending Staircases Pattern 21
Descending Staircases Pattern 22
Bump and Run Pattern 23
Triple Top Pattern 24
Triple Bottom Pattern 25
Conclusion 27

Introduction

In the fast-paced world of financial markets, understanding and analyzing trading patterns is essential for success in both cryptocurrency (crypto) and forex trading. The ability to recognize and interpret these patterns can provide traders with valuable insights into market trends, potential price movements, and optimal entry and exit points for their trades. This book aims to delve deep into the intricate world of crypto and forex trading patterns, equipping traders with the knowledge and skills necessary to navigate these volatile markets with confidence and precision.

Head and Shoulders Pattern

1. **Head and Shoulders Pattern** The Head and Shoulders pattern is a bearish reversal pattern that occurs when an asset's price forms three successive peaks, with the middle peak (the neckline) being higher than the other two.

Left Shoulder: The pattern starts with an uptrend, forming the left shoulder with a high point.

Head: The price then rises to form the head, which is higher than the left shoulder.

Right Shoulder: After the head, there is a decline in price, followed by a smaller rally forming the right shoulder, which is similar in height to the left shoulder.

Neckline: The neckline is drawn by connecting the lows of the two troughs between the peaks.

Traders often look for specific criteria when identifying a Head and Shoulders pattern, such as volume confirmation and symmetry between the shoulders. Once the price breaks below the neckline after forming the right shoulder, it is considered a signal that a trend reversal may occur.

Inverse Head and Shoulders Pattern

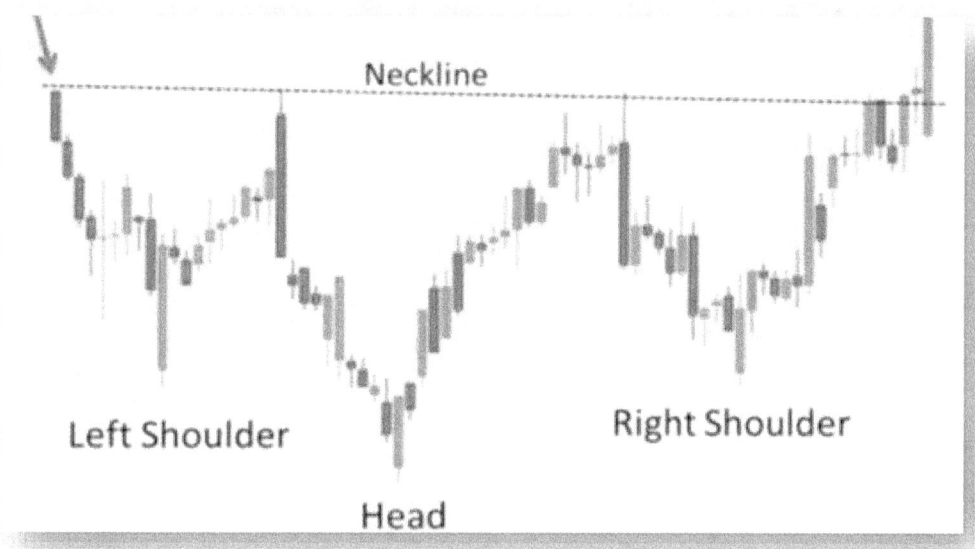

2. Inverse Head and Shoulders Pattern The Inverse Head and Shoulders pattern is a bullish reversal pattern that occurs when an asset's price forms three successive troughs, with the middle trough (the neckline) being lower than the other two.

Left Shoulder: The price reaches a low point and then bounces back up.

Head: The price drops further after the left shoulder, forming a lower low, before bouncing back up again.

Right Shoulder: Another low is formed, but this time it is higher than the head's low. The price then rises again.

The neckline of the pattern is drawn by connecting the highs between the left shoulder and the head, and then extending it to the right shoulder. Once the price breaks above this neckline, it is considered a bullish signal.

Traders often look for increased volume when the price breaks above the neckline to confirm the validity of the pattern. The projected price target after the breakout is usually calculated by measuring the distance from the head to the neckline and adding that length to the breakout point.

It's important to note that not all Inverse Head and Shoulders patterns lead to successful reversals, so it's essential to consider other technical indicators and factors before making trading decisions based solely on this pattern.

Double Top Pattern

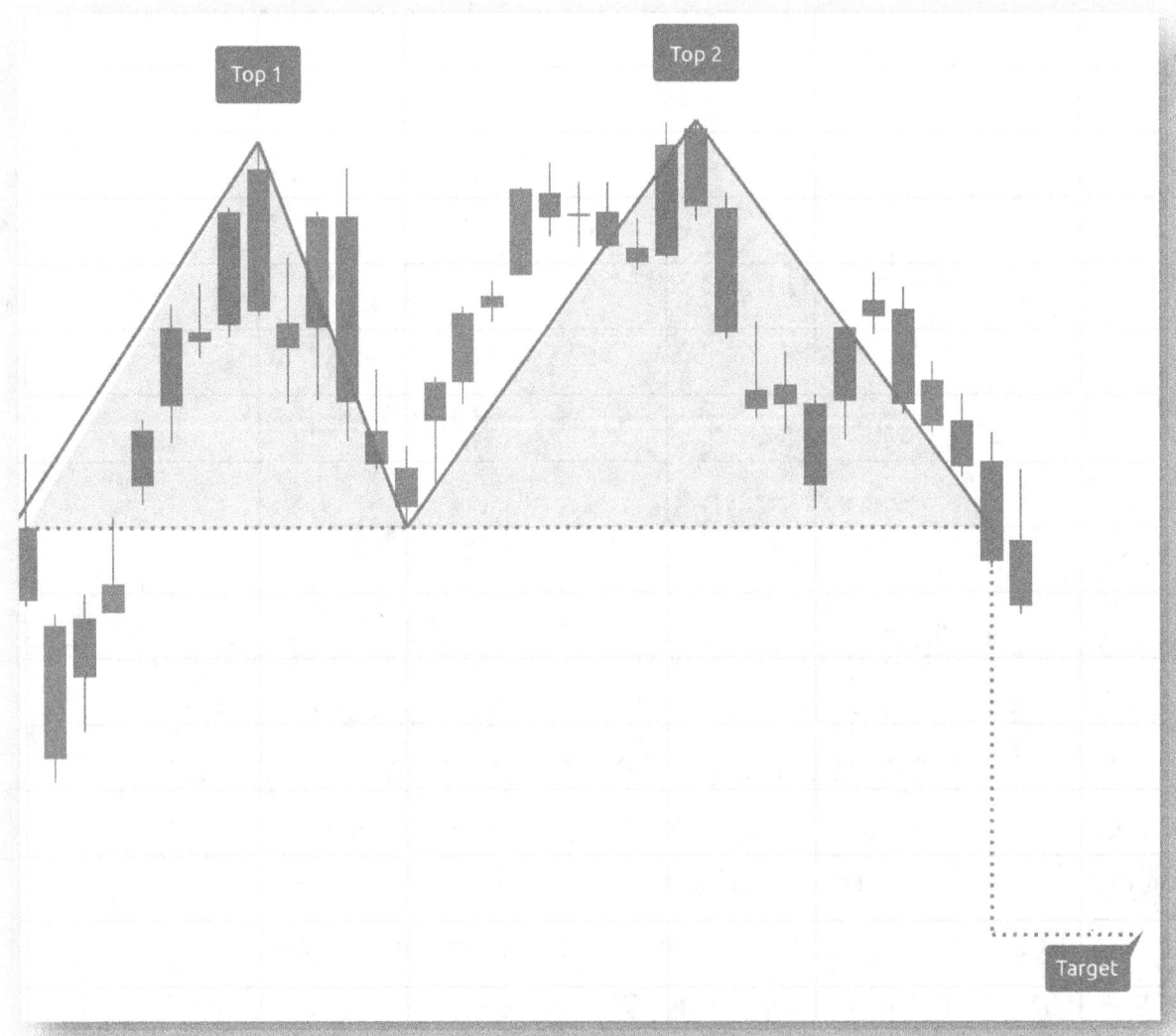

3. Double Top and Double Bottom Patterns Both Double Top and Double Bottom patterns are reversal patterns that indicate a possible change in the trend. A Double Top occurs when an asset's price forms two successive peaks at the same level.

Double Bottom Pattern

3a. A Double Bottom occurs when an asset's price forms two successive troughs at the same level.

In technical analysis, these patterns are used by traders to identify potential entry and exit points in the market. They are considered significant because they reflect shifts in market sentiment and can provide insights into future price movements.

Symmetrical Triangle Pattern

4. Triangle Patterns Triangle patterns are continuation patterns that occur when an asset's price forms a series of higher highs and higher lows (ascending triangle) or lower highs and lower lows (descending triangle).

4a. Symmetrical Triangle Pattern:

A symmetrical triangle pattern is formed when the trendlines connecting the peaks and troughs converge at a common point, with the upper trendline sloping downwards and the lower trendline sloping upwards. This pattern indicates that buyers and sellers are in equilibrium, with neither side having a clear advantage. As the triangle becomes narrower, it suggests that a breakout is imminent. The direction of the breakout can be determined by observing the prior trend before the triangle was formed. If the price was in an uptrend before the triangle, it is more likely to break out to the upside. Conversely, if the price was in a downtrend before the triangle, it is more likely to break out to the downside.

Descending Triangle Pattern

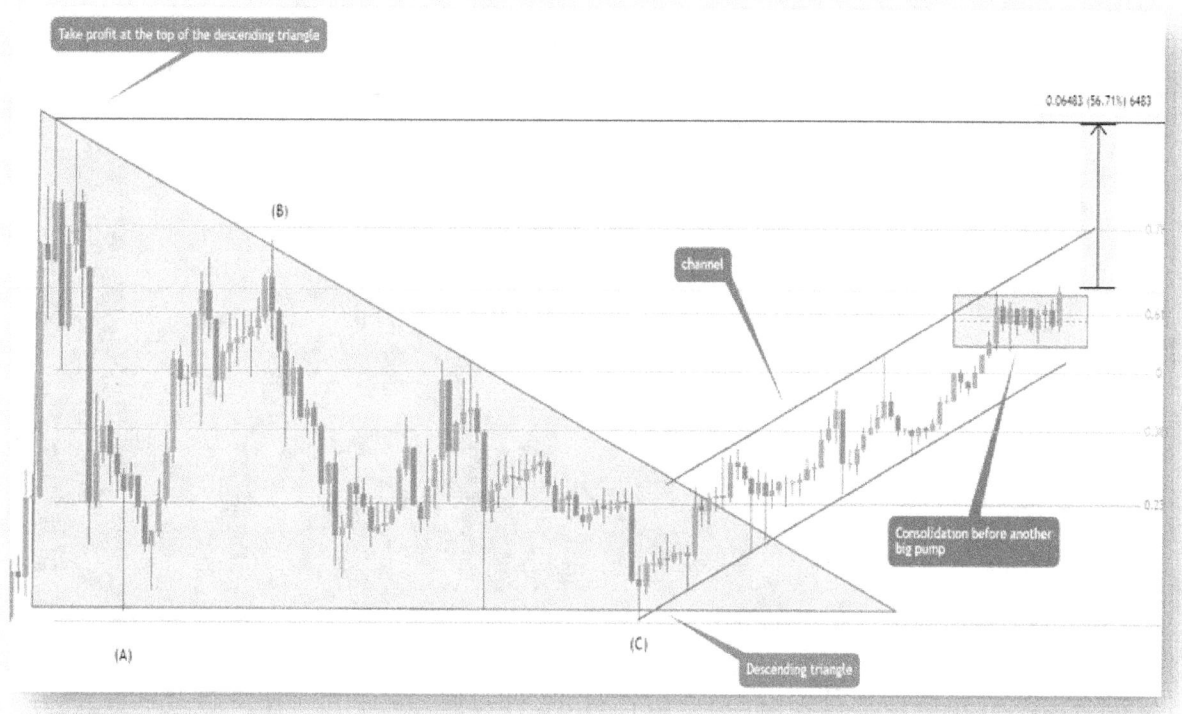

4b. Descending Triangle Pattern:

A descending triangle pattern is formed when the upper trendline slopes downwards and the lower trendline is horizontal or nearly horizontal. This pattern suggests that sellers are becoming more aggressive, but buyers are still able to keep the price from falling significantly. A descending triangle is generally considered bearish and may indicate that a breakout to the downside is imminent.

Ascending Triangle Pattern

4c. Ascending Triangle Pattern:

An ascending triangle pattern is formed when the lower trendline slopes upwards and the upper trendline is horizontal or nearly horizontal. This pattern suggests that buyers are becoming more aggressive, but sellers are still able to keep the price from rising significantly. An ascending triangle is generally considered bullish and may indicate that a breakout to the upside is imminent.

Triangle patterns can be useful for traders looking for potential entry and exit points in their trades.

Flag Pattern

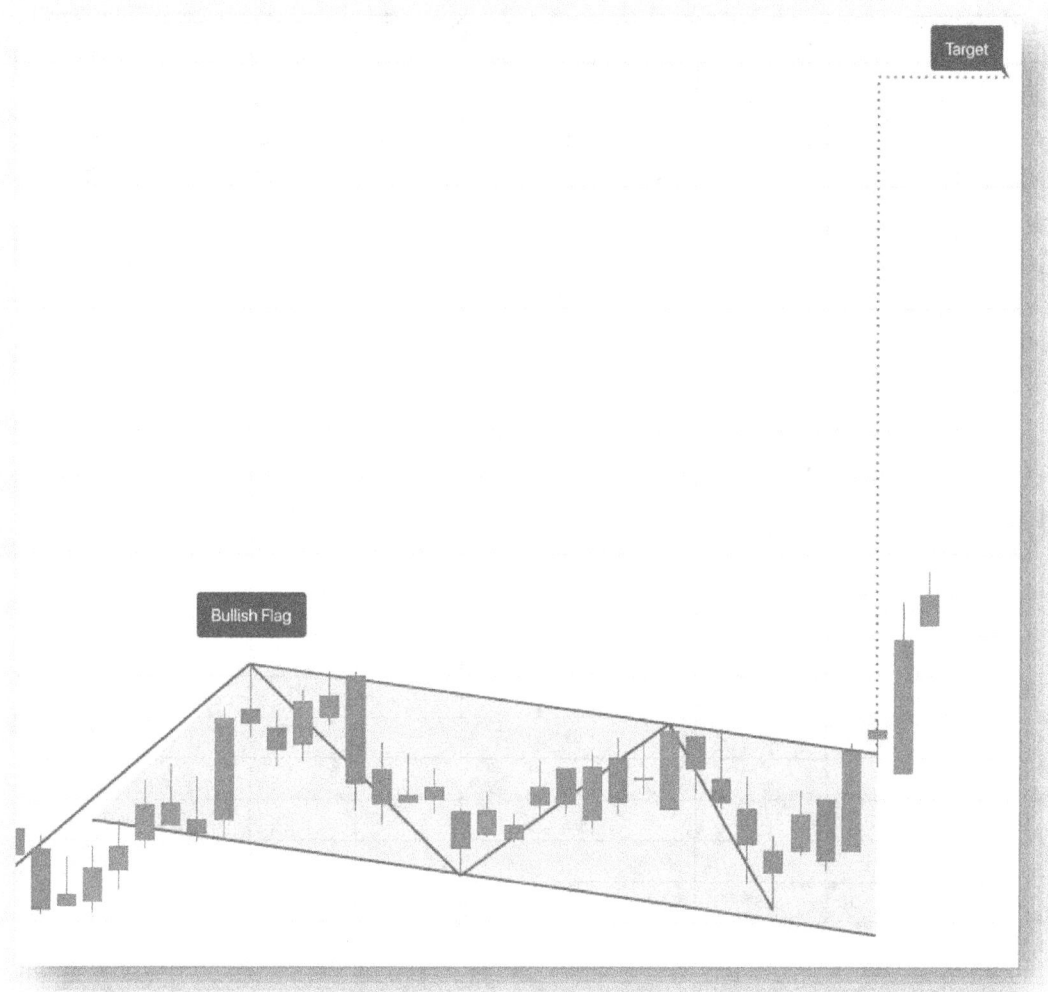

5. Flag and Pennant Patterns Flag and Pennant patterns are continuation patterns that occur when an asset's price consolidates after a strong move. A Flag pattern has a straight, flat consolidation.

Flag pattern:

Identify the initial strong move: Look for a strong advance or decline in price that covers a significant distance. This will form the "pole" of the Flag pattern.

Identify the consolidation phase: After the initial move, look for a period of consolidation where the price moves within a channel. This will form the "flag" of the pattern.

Draw the trendlines: Draw two parallel trendlines that encompass the consolidation phase. The upper trendline should slope against the direction of the trend, while the lower trendline should slope with the trend.

Wait for a breakout: The Flag pattern is complete when the price breaks out of the channel in the direction of the initial move.

Pennant Pattern

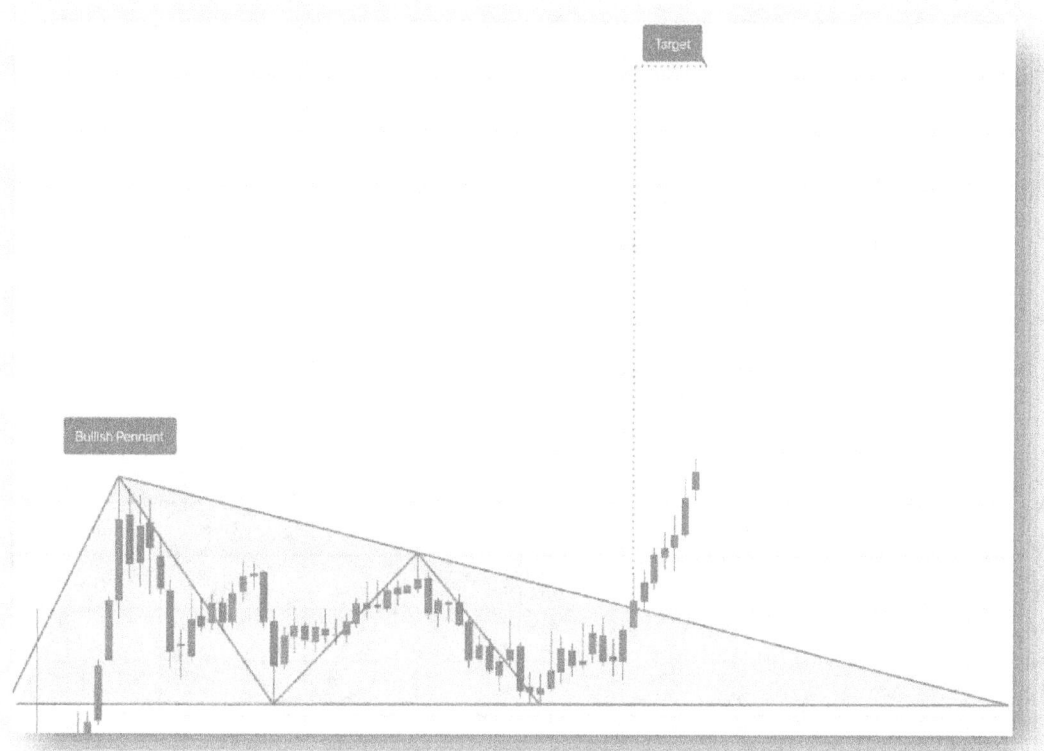

5b. A Pennant pattern has a more narrow, wedge-shaped consolidation.

Pennant pattern:

Identify the initial strong move: Look for a strong advance or decline in price that covers a significant distance. This will form the "pole" of the Pennant pattern.

Identify the consolidation phase: After the initial move, look for a period of consolidation where the price moves within a triangle or pennant shape. This will form the "pennant" of the pattern.

Draw the trendlines: Draw two converging trendlines that encompass the consolidation phase. The upper trendline should slope against the direction of the trend, while the lower trendline should slope with the trend.Wait for a breakout: The Pennant pattern is complete when the price breaks out of the triangle or pennant shape in the direction of the initial move.

Gartley Pattern

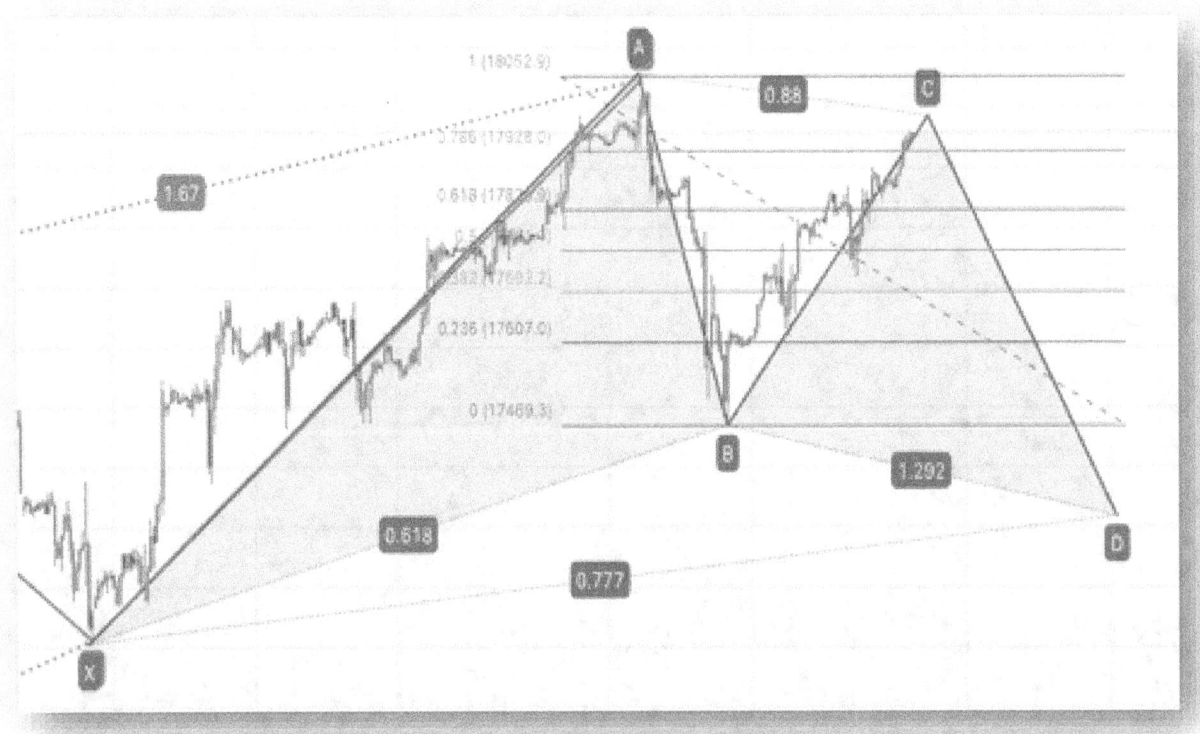

6. Gartley Butterfly Patterns Gartley and Butterfly patterns are both harmonic patterns that use Fibonacci ratios to predict potential price movements. The Gartley pattern consists of five specific price levels.

Butterfly Pattern

6b. The Butterfly pattern consists of four price levels.

To draw a Butterfly pattern, traders follow a similar process as with the Gartley pattern by identifying key Fibonacci levels and plotting the XA, AB, BC, and CD legs on the price chart. Traders look for specific ratios between these legs to confirm the validity of the pattern. Once the Butterfly pattern is recognized, traders can use it to anticipate potential trend reversals and make informed trading decisions.

Wedge Pattern

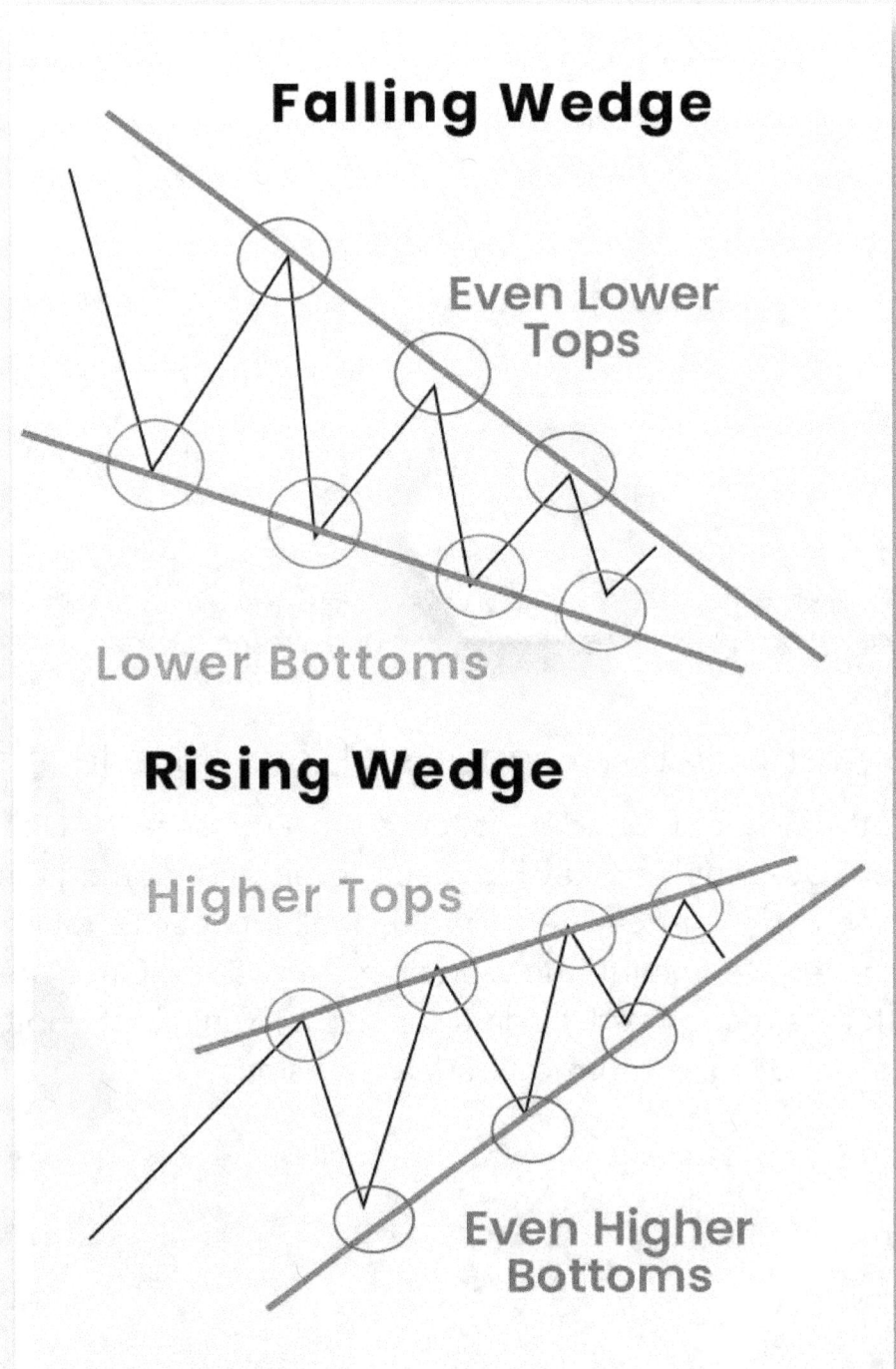

7. Wedge Pattern
The Wedge pattern is a continuation pattern that occurs when an asset's price forms a series of higher highs and higher lows (rising wedge) or lower highs and lower lows (falling wedge).

There are two types of wedge patterns:

Rising Wedge Pattern: This pattern is formed when there is a series of higher highs and higher lows, creating an upward sloping trendline as the support level and a downward sloping trendline as the resistance level. This pattern indicates a bullish trend, but as the trendlines converge, it suggests that the price movement is losing momentum and may reverse.

Falling Wedge Pattern: This pattern is formed when there is a series of lower highs and lower lows, creating a downward sloping trendline as the resistance level and an upward sloping trendline as the support level. This pattern indicates a bearish trend, but as the trendlines converge, it suggests that the price movement is losing momentum and may reverse.

Rounding Bottom Pattern

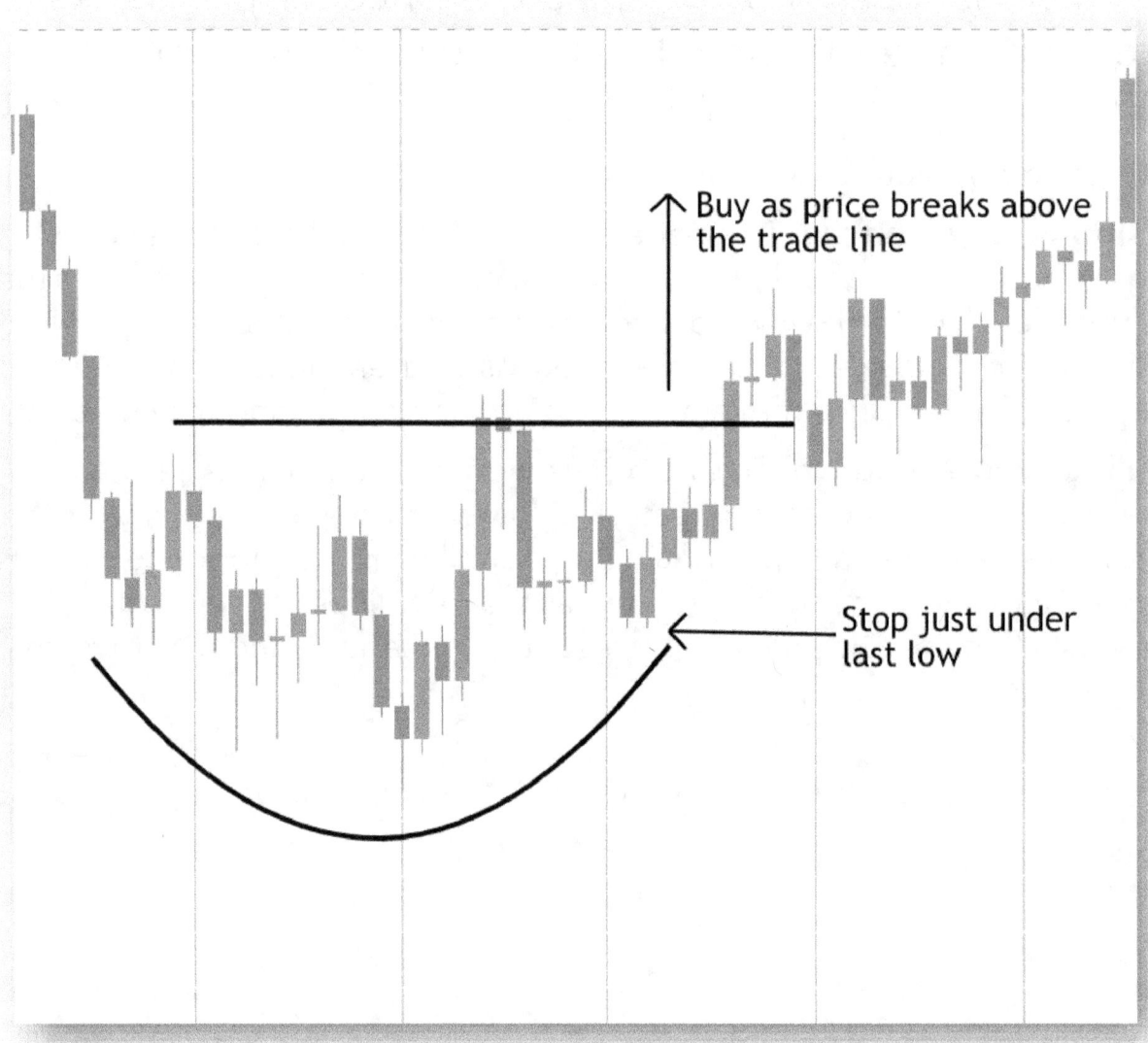

8. Rounding Bottom and Top Patterns

Rounding Bottom and Top patterns are reversal patterns that indicate a possible change in the trend. A Rounding Bottom occurs when an asset's price forms a series of higher lows and higher highs,

Identify the trend: The first step in drawing a rounding bottom or top pattern is to identify the existing trend. A rounding bottom pattern will occur in a downward trend, while a rounding top pattern will occur in an upward trend.

Look for the U-shape: The next step is to look for the U-shaped pattern that characterizes these chart patterns. In a rounding bottom pattern, the price will gradually move lower before starting to rebound and move higher. In a rounding top pattern, the price will gradually move higher before starting to decline and move lower.

Identify the resistance or support levels: In a rounding bottom pattern, the resistance level is the level at which the price has been unable to break through as it moves higher. In a rounding top pattern, the support level is the level at which the price has been unable to break through as it moves lower.

Connect the peaks or troughs: To complete the rounding bottom or top pattern, you will need to connect the peaks or troughs that make up the U-shape of the chart pattern. This will help you visualize the direction of the trend and identify any potential breakouts or breakdowns that may occur as a result of the chart pattern.

Confirm the chart pattern: It's important to note that not all U-shaped patterns will result in a rounding bottom or top chart pattern. To confirm that you are dealing with one of these chart patterns, you will need to wait for the price to break through either the resistance or support level that was established during the formation of the chart pattern.

Rounding Top Pattern

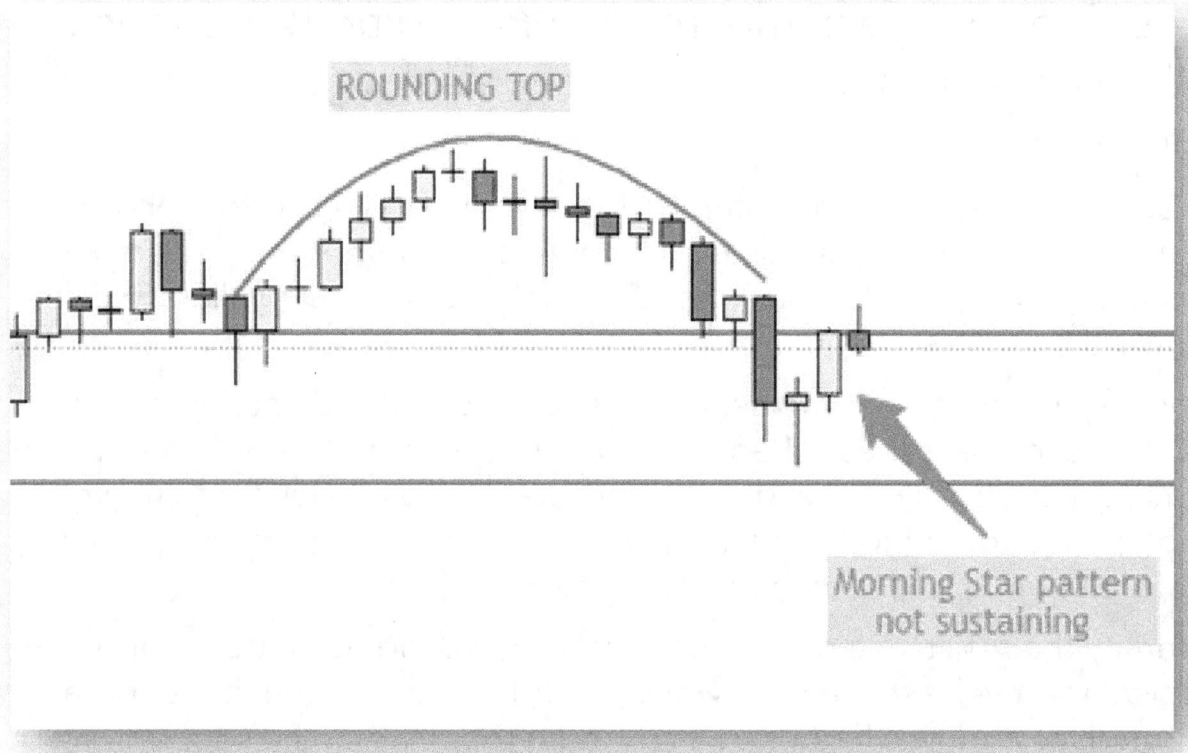

8b. A Rounding Top occurs when an asset's price forms a series of lower highs and lower lows.

Cup and Handle Pattern

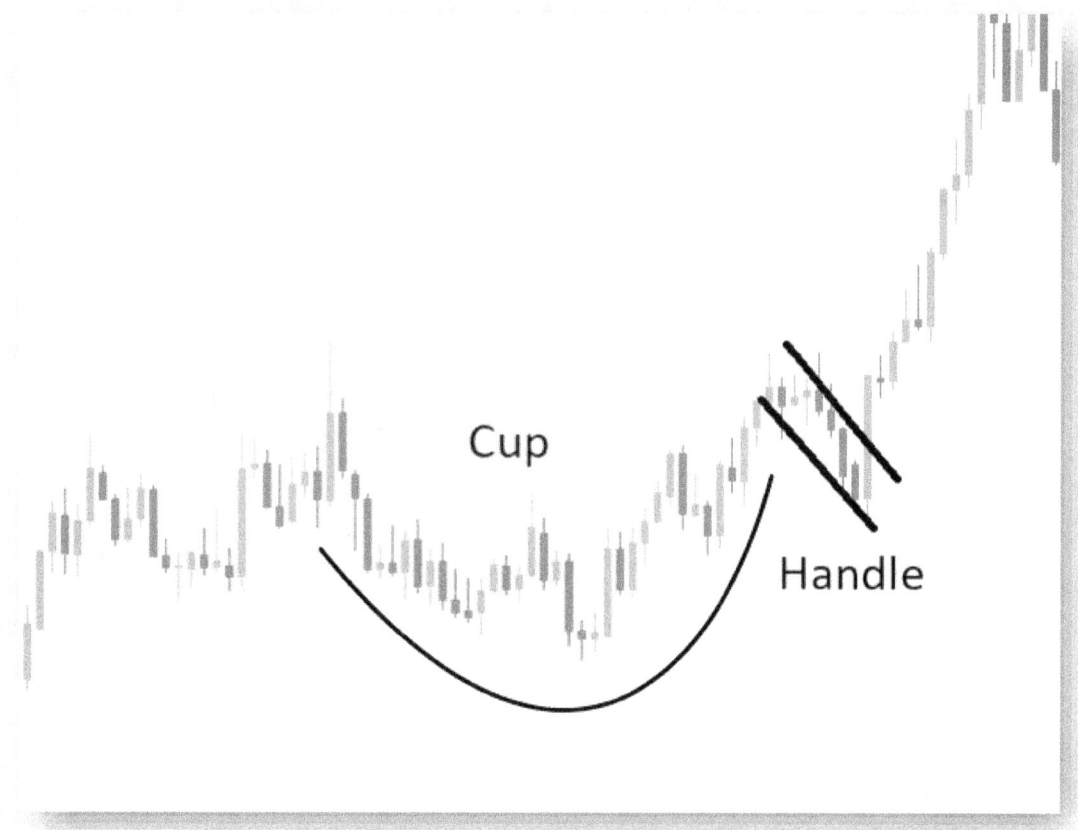

9. Cup and Handle Pattern The Cup and Handle pattern is a bullish reversal pattern that occurs when an asset's price forms a U-shaped pattern (the "cup") followed by a shorter, narrower consolidation phase (the "handle").

Cup Formation: The cup should have a rounded bottom with a gradual decrease in price followed by a gradual increase forming the right side of the cup. The depth of the cup should not be too deep or too shallow.

Handle Formation: After the cup formation, there should be a small downward price movement forming the handle. This part usually takes the shape of a small downward-sloping channel or a sideways consolidation.

Breakout: The breakout occurs when the price moves above the resistance level formed by the top of the cup. This signals a potential buying opportunity as it indicates that the uptrend is likely to continue.

Channel Pattern

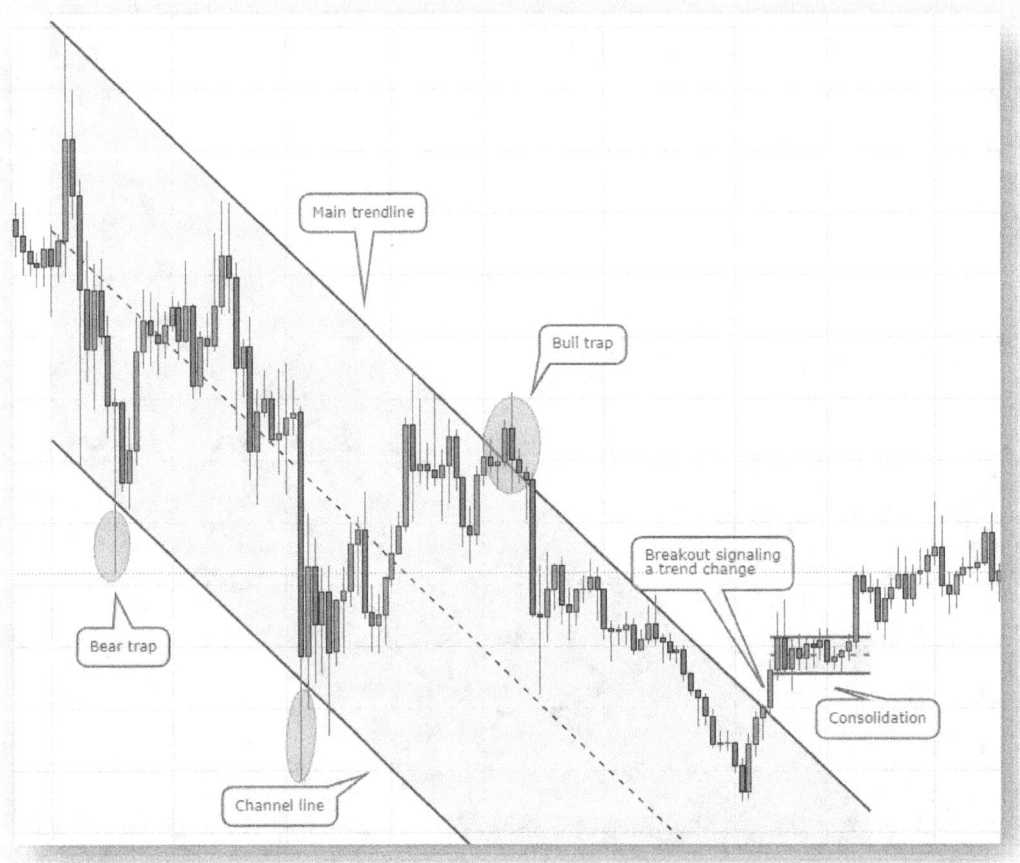

10. Channel Pattern The Channel pattern is a trend-following pattern that occurs when an asset's price moves within a parallel upward (uptrend) or downward (downtrend) channel.

It consists of two parallel trendlines that encompass the price movement of an asset, creating a channel where the price tends to fluctuate between the support and resistance levels.

Traders often use channel patterns to determine entry and exit points for trades. When the price reaches the support level in an upward channel, traders may consider buying, while selling opportunities arise when the price approaches the resistance level in a downward channel. Additionally, breakouts from the channel pattern can signal potential trend reversals or continuations, providing valuable insights for traders.

Ascending Staircases Pattern

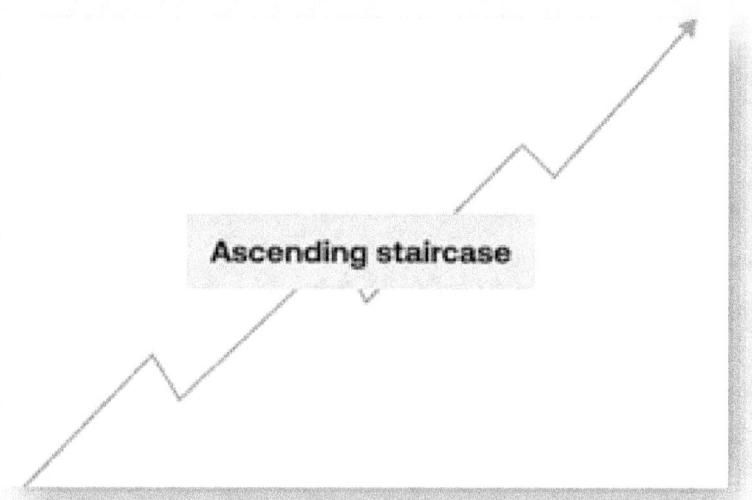

11. Ascending Staircases. Ascending and descending staircases are probably the most basic chart patterns. But they're still important to know if you're interested in identifying and trading trends.

Take a look at any market, and you'll notice that price action is rarely linear. Even in strong uptrends and downtrends, you'll see some movement against the prevailing momentum.

In an ascending staircase, a market is moving upwards. While it retraces occasionally, it is still hitting higher highs and the lows are getting higher too. This is what a bull market generally looks like, and traders will consider going long until the uptrend comes to an end.

The dips in the trend can even provide useful buying opportunities, enabling you to get in on the rally at a discount.

Descending Staircases Pattern

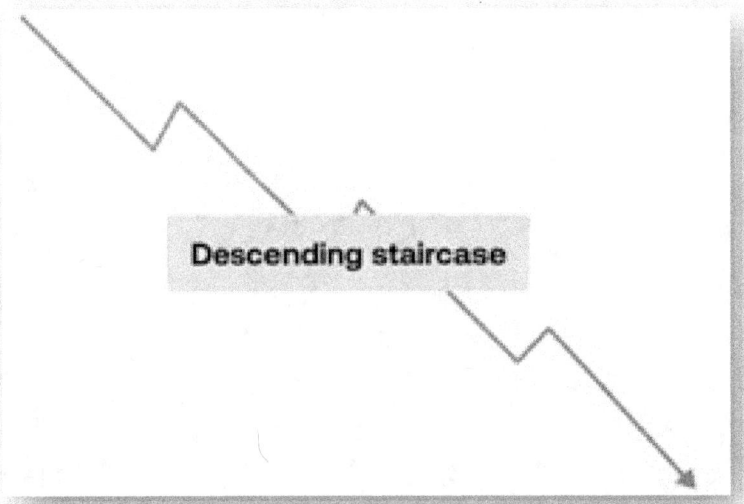

11a. Descending Staircases. When markets are forming lower lows and lower highs this can be considered a downtrend and forms a descending staircase. In this phase, traders would consider trading on the short side of the market. And in a downtrend, a trader could use the mini rallies that go against the bear run as opportunities to sell.

Bump and Run Pattern

12. The Bump and Run pattern is a technical analysis chart pattern commonly used in trading to identify potential changes in the direction of a security's price movement. This pattern consists of two phases: the bump phase and the run phase.

Bump Phase: In the bump phase, the price of the security experiences a sharp increase, creating a peak that resembles a bump on the chart. This rapid rise in price is often driven by strong buying pressure or positive market sentiment.

Run Phase: Following the bump phase, the price of the security retraces slightly before continuing its upward trend. During this run phase, the price gradually increases as buyers continue to dominate the market.

Traders use the Bump and Run pattern to anticipate potential trend reversals or breakouts. The pattern suggests that after a significant increase in price, there may be a period of consolidation or retracement before another upward movement

Triple Top Pattern

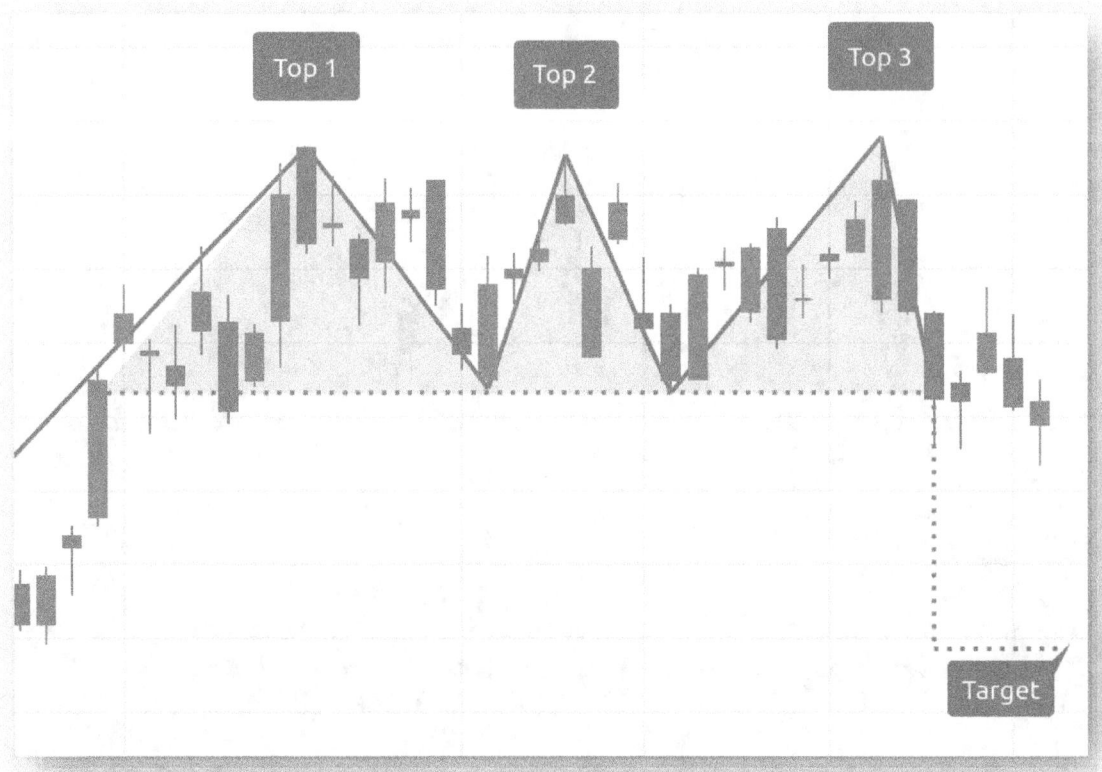

13. The Triple Top Pattern is a technical analysis chart pattern that signals a potential reversal of an uptrend. It is considered a bearish reversal pattern and is formed when the price of an asset creates three peaks at approximately the same level, followed by a decline below the support level. The pattern is characterized by three consecutive peaks that fail to break above a certain resistance level, creating a line known as the "neckline."

Traders and analysts often look for the Triple Top Pattern as an indication that the uptrend may be losing momentum and that a trend reversal to the downside could be imminent. The pattern is confirmed when the price breaks below the neckline, which acts as a support level. This breakout is seen as a signal to sell or short the asset, with the expectation that prices will continue to decline.

Triple Bottom Pattern

14. The Triple Bottom pattern is a bullish reversal pattern that forms in a downtrend and can signal the potential end of the trend and the beginning of an uptrend.

It is called a "Triple Bottom" because it consists of three price troughs that are roughly equal, with each trough representing a failed attempt to break below the previous low.

The pattern begins with a downward trend, where the price makes lower highs and lower lows. At some point, the downtrend slows down, and the price starts to form a series of three consecutive bottoms at roughly the same level. These bottoms are typically separated by small rallies, which fail to push the price above the previous high. The pattern is complete when the price breaks through the resistance level formed by the highs of these rallies.

Here are some key characteristics of the Triple Bottom pattern:

It forms over a period of time, typically several weeks or months, as the price consolidates and forms three distinct bottoms.

The three bottoms should be roughly equal in price level, indicating strong support at this level.

Each bottom should be accompanied by a corresponding rally, which fails to push the price above the previous high.

The pattern is confirmed when the price breaks through the resistance level formed by the highs of these rallies.

Volume should decrease during each bottom and increase during each subsequent rally, indicating decreasing selling pressure and increasing buying pressure.

The Triple Bottom pattern is considered a bullish reversal pattern because it indicates that buyers are becoming more aggressive at lower price levels, eventually overpowering sellers and pushing the price upwards.

Conclusion

In conclusion, understanding and recognizing trading patterns is crucial for successful trading in the financial markets. By analyzing historical data, traders can identify trends, support and resistance levels, and potential entry and exit points. The various types of trading patterns discussed in this book, such as head and shoulders, triangles, channels, and flags, provide valuable insights into market behavior and can help traders make informed decisions.

However, it is essential to remember that no trading pattern is foolproof, and markets are constantly evolving. Traders must be adaptable and open to adjusting their strategies based on new information and market conditions. Risk management is also paramount, as even the most experienced traders can experience losses.

www.ingramcontent.com/pod-product-compliance
Lightning Source LLC
Chambersburg PA
CBHW062237220526
45471CB00009B/3520